www.MillenniumPublishingLimited.com

Marriage Counseling Workbook

For Couples

20

Ways To Rekindle The

Love In Your Marriage

By

Dr. Jane Smart

www.MillenniumPublishingLimited.com

www.MillenniumPublishingLimited.com

Copyright ©2019

All rights reserved. Except as permitted under the U.S. Copyright Act of 1976, the scanning, uploading and distribution of this book via the Internet or via any other means without the express permission of the author is illegal and punishable by law. Please purchase only authorized electronic editions, and do not participate in or encourage electronic piracy of copyrighted material.

Disclaimer

This publication is designed to provide competent and reliable information regarding the subject matter covered. However, it is sold with the understanding that the author is not engaged in rendering relationship or other professional advice. Laws and practices often vary from state to state and country to country and if expert assistance is required, the services of a professional should be sought. The author specifically disclaims any liability that is incurred from the use or application of the contents of this book.

Other Books By Dr. Jane Smart

The Simple Pregnancy Guide

Strong Woman: What It Means To Be A Woman Of Substance

Bonus Offer

The kindle edition will be available to you for FREE when you purchase the paperback version from Amazon.com (The US Store)

Table of Contents

Introduction 7

Respect Individuality 12

Lead With Kindness 17

Go on a Date 24

Be Attractive 30

Don't Take Your Partner for Granted 36

Don't Be Snarky 39

Touch More Often 41

Rediscover Sexual Pleasures 45

Have Fun Together 49

Take a Vacation 52

Practice Emotional Intimacy 54

Share and Reinforce Memories 57

Practice Acceptance and Tolerance 60

Compliment Your Spouse 62

Keep Communication Channels Open 65

Break the Rules 70

Honor Your Spouse's Preferences 72

Make Your Spouse Happy 74

Don't Argue in Anger 77
Limit Technology 80
Have A Happy Married Life! 86
The End 89

Introduction

"We are all born for love. It is the principle of existence, and its only end."

– Benjamin Disraeli

This book's goal is to protect the beauty and joy of married life and help couples to rekindle the love in a dying marriage.

For many couples, the wonderfully positive aspects of marriage have become lost amid the monotony, pressures, and challenges of daily life.

Take marriage seriously as a lifetime promise while also committing to make that shared lifetime one of joy and happiness rather than boredom or bitterness.

Do you remember the delight you experienced when you first met and fell in love with the person you married? Did you feel giddy and eager for your next time together? Did you replay the date afterwards in your head? Did he or she treat you like royalty and make you feel special? Did you have a big, bright smile on your face and butterflies in your stomach?

You each realized you had found the romantic partner you may have dreamed about since you were a child. The two of you decided to get married because you wanted those feelings to last for the rest of your life. You happily committed to spending your lives together as a couple.

After many years of marriage, though, you noticed that the happiness, joy, and romance were fading away and that the physical intimacy was decreasing. The traits and habits of your partner that used to amuse you now leave you angry and irritated. The differences between the two of you that you found so attractive now separate you from your spouse.

It is time to rekindle the love in your marriage. Love is an essential element of a good marriage; couples must find a way to rekindle their love if it starts to fade. You need love, passion, romance, and physical intimacy just as much now as when you were a newlywed.

If you are coping with this loss of love by screaming at your spouse or using the silent treatment, how is that working out for you? If the two of you are tired of an unsatisfactory relationship and seek a way out, do not assume the way out requires throwing in the towel and starting over with another partner.

If you have wondered where the joy, great sex, fun times, romance, and intimacy have disappeared, take that as an urgent signal that it is time to rekindle the love you have for each other and to save your marriage from crumbling into divorce.

Rekindling love in a marriage requires cooperation between you and your spouse. This book offers practical suggestions for finding the love that might have been lost over time.

Before you start reading this book and putting the suggestions into practice, be very honest with yourself about whether you actually want your marriage to work out well, if you really want to stay with your spouse, and if you truly anticipate a relationship of joy and happiness with your spouse.

If the answer is NO, find a professional marriage counselor to assist you as you explore whether to move on or stay in the marriage.

If the answer is YES, this book if for you. Read on and enjoy the book.

The first basic principle to keep in mind if you want to rekindle the love in your marriage is to treat your relationship with your spouse as more important than any other thing in your life. It needs to be more important than work, friends, parents, technology, hobbies, egos, and children.

Being in a happy relationship provides important benefits. For instance, couples in happy marriages have better health compared to their single or divorced counterparts.

You and your spouse might have grown apart as the stress of work and kids reduced the spark of love in your marriage. If you are ready to reignite the flame of love in your marriage, let's get started.

Respect Individuality

"Love… What is love? Love is to love someone for who they are, who they were, and who they will be." **–Chris Moore**

You and your spouse are unique individuals with different feelings, beliefs, likes and dislikes, desires, habits, dreams, and goals. We have an inborn right to be who we are. We all hope to express our true selves freely with our partner.

You should not expect your spouse to change into someone else after saying 'I do.' It also is unrealistic and burdensome to expect your spouse to meet all of your needs or to view the world the way you view it.

You are two different individuals with different backgrounds and experiences brought together through love and your pledge to live together forever.

What you expect from your partner and how you treat him or her should reflect acceptance. Respect your partner for who she is, not who you want her to be—just as you want acceptance from her without the need to change. Find a way to resolve differences thoughtfully. When you love your spouse who he is, you are acknowledging his authentic self.

You should not question why your spouse needs what she needs. If a child gets up in the middle of the night and says he is thirsty, would you tell the boy that he really is not thirsty and send him back to bed?

The key to making your marriage flourish is to appreciate your spouse's individuality. Your spouse is not your clone. Why would you expect him to react exactly the way you react?

Study your partner to understand why she acts the way she does. Seeking understanding can minimize conflict, boost trust, and make your marriage more satisfying and fulfilling.

One foundation of your marriage is the mutual adoration and love you have for each other, but you cannot expect everything to be all roses all the time—especially if you don't feed the rose bed.

You and your spouse will have some fundamental differences; any time people live together, whether as romantic partners, family members, or housemates, they will disagree at times.

How can you maintain the love in your marriage when you and your partner have conflicting interests and points of view? Stay unprejudiced and nonjudgmental as you and your spouse discuss your differences.

You each should know the other's feelings about children, family, household management, finances, decision-making, technology usage, and problem-solving techniques. Discuss long-term goals, hopes, dreams, and aspirations with your spouse.

True love is the ability to love your spouse as he is in his essence. If you desire a positive relationship for a lifetime with the person you fell in love with, you must see her as a unique individual and not as an extension of yourself.

Loving someone who loves you in return is an amazing experience. To nurture that love, accept that your partner may be different from you in many ways, that the two of you will not view the world the same way, and that you may not share the same habits or beliefs. Accept and honor these differences because they helped create the unique person you love.

Other Books By Dr. Jane Smart

<u>The Simple Pregnancy Guide</u>
<u>Strong Woman: What It Means To Be A Woman Of Substance</u>

Bonus Offer

The kindle edition will be available to you for FREE when you purchase the paperback version from Amazon.com (The US Store)

Lead With Kindness

"Kindness is THE miracle cure that will help all kinds of marriage and relationship problems." –

Anonymous

A simple act of kindness can rekindle the love in your marriage. To resolve conflicts and reignite love more quickly, start by being respectful and kind toward your spouse.

Daily acts of kindness lead to positivity and happiness, which are essential for a lifetime relationship of joy. According to some relationship experts, for a marriage to last, we need five positive interactions to balance one negative interaction. A marriage is in danger of crashing when the ratio of positive to negative interactions goes below five to one.

Even when you feel angry or upset with your spouse, you still can be kind. Guard against being overtly unkind in disagreements. Avoid speaking condescendingly or making disparaging remarks to your spouse. To transform your relationships, consciously choose kindness in your interactions with everyone—especially your spouse.

Kindness is the key to closeness, intimacy, friendship and love. Kindness is the lubricant to keep your marriage running optimally; kindness can make your marriage successful no matter what else happens. A dose of kindness applied frequently is a great prescription for improving your marriage.

Why is kindness so important?

When you and your spouse said yes to marriage, you believed that you would be kind to each other. If you were not convinced of that, why would you agree to a lifetime relationship together?

Imagine two business people exploring a joint venture. If one of the partners suspects that the other partner will eventually defraud him, why would he go forward with the partnership?

This is also true for a marriage. If you or your lover had noticed that kindness was missing from your courtship, you likely would have ended the relationship before making a more serious commitment.

You and your spouse married believing that the kindness you showed to each other during the dating and courtship period would last forever.

The two of you can find countless ways to behave kindly to each other. This following saying is a cliché because it is true: "The more you give the more you get."

In a non-abusive relationship, if you show love to your partner, your partner will behave lovingly toward you too. If you respect your partner, your partner will behave respectfully toward you too. If you treat your partner with kindness, you will receive kindness.

Religious leaders and philosophers have taught us that considering how we would like to be treated can guide us in how we treat others.

The prescription has various phrasings, including the Golden Rule of "Do unto others what you would have them do unto you." as well as "Don't do unto others what you don't want others to do unto you."

Living by this rule can be the accelerant that rekindles the love in your marriage. When you need to make a choice or take action that affects your mate, think about what you would want your partner to do in a role reversal.

Lack of kindness in a marriage is a never-ending source of marital problems. Behaviors opposite to kindness include anger, physical assault, irresponsibility and selfishness, criticism, disrespect, and cheating.

A happy marriage begins with kindness, and kindness sustains it. If the love in your marriage has pulled a disappearing act, kindness probably vanished first; it is now time to bring kindness back into your marriage.

Think about ten behaviors that will make your spouse feel loved and cared for. Write these ten actions on paper or commit them to memory. Now begin performing all the behaviors with good intentions.

After doing this for several days, you will be amazed by how much the love in your marriage has blossomed. This little exercise can significantly rekindle the love between the two of you. You and your partner will experience the miracle cure of kindness.

However, kindness may not work if you or your partner cannot let go of the past and start afresh. Kindness creates the fertile soil in which affection, love, and passion can grow. Kindness is a foundation upon which to build or rebuild a happy marriage.

It is very easy to be kind, but it may be difficult to change if being unkind has become a habit. Once you start, you will realize that the benefits of being kind far outweigh the effort.

Kindness almost guarantees a happy married life. Each act of kindness you perform creates a positive memory for your spouse. When you hurt your spouse, whether intentionally or unintentionally, these positive memories stand as advocates in mitigating your spouse's negative judgments. This storehouse of warm feelings can help reestablish harmony in your marriage.

The more positive memories you create for your spouse, the easier it will be for your mate to overlook any intentional wounding or unintentional mistakes you make, because your partner will see them as rare exceptions to your normal kindness.

Kindness is contagious. If you are kind to your spouse, your spouse is more likely to be kind to you. Love, joy, and appreciation will grow stronger with each act of kindness.

Go on a Date

"Most people are about as happy as they make up their minds to be."

– Abraham Lincoln

Dating is not restricted to the period of courtship. It also should be a regular avenue to connect with your spouse after marriage.

You and your spouse may have more responsibilities now if you have children to care for as well as work, but you still need to have regular dates.

Start planning a regular date night with your spouse. You and your spouse may want to alternate planning the date. Surprise each other with activities that can rekindle love in your marriage.

You do not have to spend a lot of money to have a romantic date with your spouse. Always remember that when it is a matter of love, small things matter a lot. A candlelit dinner for two in a quiet place, a stroll in the moonlight, or a summer picnic can be a wonderful date night.

If life's responsibilities and demands have pushed your marriage to the bottom of your priority list, you and your spouse need to plan deliberately so that you can share quality time together.

Be creative with your date and make sure you have fun, just as you did when you were still courting. Take responsibility for rekindling the love in your marriage. Anticipating and remembering a date extends the pleasure.

Redefine date night with your spouse. Create a regular time to be together as a couple, a time away from jobs, kids, church, and other responsibilities. Use this date time to reconnect with your spouse and to remember the love that brought you together.

You and your spouse should determine what is romantic to both of you. Your date can be as simple as having a heart-based conversation during a walk together.

Dating allows you to see your spouse as the lover you are building your life with rather than as a co-homeowner or a co-parent.

The relationship between you and your spouse forms the foundation of your family, so when this foundation begins to crumble, other things can crumble as well. Making time for each other strengthens that foundation.

Dating time is a time to get away with your spouse so that you can talk, have fun, and laugh together. It is a time to learn more about each other and to share your dreams for the future. This rekindles the love in your relationship.

Your spouse deserves more than the leftover minutes of your life. Give your spouse premium access to your time and put your soulmate at the top of your priority list.

You need to plan your date ahead of time to make sure it happens. Waiting until the last minute leaves too much to chance. You also can reconnect daily in shorter blocks of time by playing a game, talking, or watching a favorite show or a movie together.

If you find it difficult to plan a date, start simply:

- Reminisce about what you and your spouse most enjoyed doing together during courtship. Start scheduling those activities again.

- Think about the activities your spouse loves. Try doing those activities together. Involve your spouse in your own activities when you can.

- Think of a new activity that you and your spouse can try together.

The main point is for you and your spouse to spend some time together without the distractions of your day-to-day life.

Consider these important points as you begin dating your spouse again:

1. Have the right perspective. You and your spouse both need to recognize that spending time together should be a priority. You need to acknowledge that regular dating will rekindle the love in your marriage.

2. Make a commitment. Do not think of a date as a quick fix. Having a regular date with your spouse is only the start. You also maintain the love in your marriage by constantly being aware of your spouse's emotional needs and striving to meet those needs.

Do not stop the practice just because you went on a few dates, your spouse is now happier with you, or you are running out of date night ideas. These are not valid reasons to stop dating your spouse.

3. Apply creativity to dating. You do not need to plan expensive or elaborate dates. A date is just special time together for you and your spouse. This is what dating is all about. Be creative and plan something interesting and fun.

Be Attractive

*"Everyone should carefully observe which way his heart draws him, and then choose that way with all his strength." – **Hasidic saying***

Was the person you eventually married interested in you—at least in part—because of a physical attraction? Were you likewise physically attracted?

Did you enhance your attractiveness by spending extra time on grooming before a date? What message did that send?

To keep your marriage strong long after the honeymoon, maintain your appearance as you did when you were dating. If you stop taking care of yourself and become unattractive, are you telling your spouse without words that you do not care enough to make an effort?

While a marriage needs more than physical attraction to last, your mate's love for you may wither if your appearance sends an I-don't-care message. Your spouse may even compare you unfavorably to someone else.

Showing your spouse that you are willing to make an effort with your appearance long after the exchange of vows helps sustain the love in your marriage.

One of the basic reasons for dating someone in the first place is that we find that person attractive. Did you date many people that you considered unattractive?

Did you give a lot of thought to what you would wear and how you would look on your first date with the person you eventually married? It should not surprise you to know that physical attraction is one of the most important factors in a happy married life. Always present yourself attractively to your life partner.

As I write this book, this expression popped into my mind: "Familiarity breeds contempt." Some relaxation of effort on both sides may be expected and understandable after marriage, but this should not extend to making NO effort to take care of yourself.

It can be very difficult for your spouse to tell you that he is no longer attracted to you, knowing how hurtful this statement would be to you.

Your spouse might try to tell you indirectly about the problem. He might suggest a new outfit or invite you to the gym. She might ask you to shave or make clothing suggestions. Your mate may not be more direct through fear of hurting your feelings.

How to be attractive

1. Take care of your physical self: Regardless of your age, aim to be healthy. When you are healthy, you will look attractive to your spouse. Monitor your weight, eat a healthy diet, and get adequate exercise and sleep. You both will grow older; you should each respect normal signs of aging such as wrinkles, while not using aging as an excuse to neglect yourself.

2. Practice good hygiene: Take a bath every day, brush your teeth often, shave, and groom your hair. This shows respect for yourself, your spouse, and your marriage. No one wants to cuddle up to someone who smells and looks unattractive.

3. Dress well: Change your old shirt and dirty jeans for something nicer. Consider your spouse's preferences about how much makeup and scent you wear. Your spouse deserves a well-turned-out partner.

4. Do what your spouse loves: Wearing the perfume or hairstyle that your spouse prefers can signal that you care.

5. Stop annoying habits: While you should feel free to be yourself in your home, when you have a spouse, letting it all hang out may make you look unattractive to your mate and may cause problems in your marriage.

Other Books By Dr. Jane Smart

The Simple Pregnancy Guide

Strong Woman: What It Means To Be A Woman Of Substance

Bonus Offer

The kindle edition will be available to you for FREE when you purchase the paperback version from Amazon.com (The US Store)

Don't Take Your Partner for Granted

"Do not take anything for granted—not one smile or one person or one rainbow or one breath, or one night in your cozy bed." – **Terri Guillemets**

Taking your spouse for granted means that you do not value your spouse enough. You may be doing that by not showing appreciation when your spouse does something nice for you. You may expect your spouse to help you with something or perform a service without considering your spouse's needs or availability. You may interrupt her day constantly to ask for favors.

After marriage, you develop a sense of who your spouse is and what he or she can do. Your spouse provides support, stability, and dependability. Because of this, you may start expecting your spouse to help you with tasks outside of family life, such as your career. This is a form of taking your spouse for granted.

All of these acts or omissions can add up to disregard for your spouse's feelings. When you take your spouse for granted and take advantage of him, he might feel frustrated and resentful. To rekindle the love in your marriage, treat your spouse with gratitude instead of presuming on her goodwill

Say 'please' and 'thank you' often and appreciate your spouse for everything he does for you, be it small or big. Buy gifts for your spouse to show her you appreciate her. Create a list of things you appreciate about your spouse and show her how valuable she is to you.

Show and tell your spouse frequently how much you love him. Give your partner your undivided attention to make him feel loved and special. To rekindle the love in your marriage, express it often. Show your soulmate that you cherish her.

Follow these simple ways to make your spouse feel special:

- Send her a letter or card without needing a special occasion.

- Tell him how much you miss him and how much you crave being with him.

- Write love notes or poems for your spouse.

- Share the events of your day, and ask about her day as well—and then listen to her answer.

- Show respect by listening to your spouse whenever he or she talks to you.

- Be with your spouse in body, mind, and spirit.

Don't Be Snarky

*"Patience and perseverance have a magical effect before which difficulties disappear and obstacles vanish." – **John Quincy Adams***

Criticizing or abusing your spouse will damage your relationship and may lead to divorce. Everyone makes mistakes; harshly criticizing your spouse will push him further away from you, which makes it harder to have a happy married life.

Be your spouse's best friend. Do things to please her, not to bring her down. Make him feel happy and glad to be with you. Help him put his mistakes in perspective. Remind her that everybody goofs up at times and that it is not the end of the world.

Admire and praise your spouse much more often than you judge her or him. That does not mean you cannot occasionally provide carefully phrased constructive feedback, but avoid calling your spouse names and avoid using phrases such as 'you always' or 'you never' with your spouse.

Forget about the past; don't bring it into an argument for the sake of winning. Let bygones be bygones forever.

When you argue with your spouse—as opposed to having a reasonable discussion—neither of you wins because both of you lose the love in the marriage. This affects intimacy and creates a gap.

Fighting between you and your spouse shows immaturity regardless of the cause of the fight or the amount of time you have been married. Grow up and maintain peace to fill your relationship with love, happiness, and joy.

Touch More Often

"To keep a lamp burning we have to keep putting oil in it." – **Mother Teresa**

Always remember that a simple touch has enormous power. Touch your spouse more often:

- Hold his hand while walking or sitting together

- Hug your spouse or put your arms around her

- Cuddle together.

You can easily create warmth and love by touching your spouse. You can also rekindle love in your marriage by publicly expressing your love and affection for your spouse. A simple way to show your spouse how much you love her is to touch her several times a day.

How often do you touch your spouse? Increase the frequency of touch to strengthen your relationship.

Create an atmosphere of comfort and relaxation by touching your spouse while sitting or walking together. Touching your spouse can even alleviate pain.

Touches create a release of feel-good brain chemicals that help trigger loving feelings. A twenty-second hug from you can produce dopamine and oxytocin in your wife's brain.

Every day, before and after work, hug and kiss your spouse. This will change your hormonal level, which in turn will regenerate affection in your relationship.

Some studies actually show that frequent kissing creates better bonding and more satisfaction in a relationship than sex. A few seconds of kissing leads to release of the oxytocin, sometimes called the cuddle hormone.

Humans have hundreds of thousands of microscopic nerve endings under the skin designed to sense loving touch from our mates. A tender touch from you signifies that you care for your spouse. It can give your spouse emotional security, calmness, and comfort. The need for a tender touch is healthy rather than abnormal, and you never outgrow that need.

The present world is highly sexual; it ignores the significance of touching apart from sex and conditions us to turn only to sex when we feel a need for loving closeness with a spouse.

If you practice physical touching with your spouse in all of its pleasant nonsexual forms, you will experience a joyful marriage. Cuddling and snuggling, sleeping close to your spouse, and sharing affection by simply touching will boost the love in your marriage.

Rediscover Sexual Pleasures

"Remember, a good marriage is like a campfire. Both grow cold if left unattended." – **H. Jackson Brown, Jr.**

While increasing nonsexual touch enhances marriage, you also need to avoid letting the sex act become routine or nonexistent. Try sex in different positions, variations, and places to help rekindle love in your marriage.

A wise man once said, "Do not make love to different men or women, but make love to the same man or woman in different ways to keep the love alive in marriage and pacify the temptations of adultery." If you need information or inspiration, the internet has you covered.

Make sexual fantasies welcome in your marital bed. Be open to trying new things without feeling that you have to do anything you find repugnant or painful. Someone who cannot fulfill his or her sexual desires within the marriage may find extramarital sex more tempting. Encourage your spouse to express secret desires. Bring back the passionate love you experienced when dating by being more romantic and sexy with each other.

The fulfillment of two basic needs help build a happy marriage. We need security (knowing that our spouse has our back no matter what), and we need novelty, excitement, and mystery. As humans, we always crave having one person fulfill both of these basic needs.

Flirting with your spouse as if you had just met adds excitement to marriage. Any affectionate act can be flirtatious. The important thing is to find something that you and your spouse are comfortable with and that serves as fun for the two of you.

Sex is vital to most marriages. Animals generally mate only when the female is fertile, for the purpose of procreation; humans have sex primarily to have fun. Use sexual pleasure to rekindle the love in your marriage.

The exciting thing about the sexual act in marriage is that each of you knows what turns your spouse on and how your spouse's body works—or at least you should! Great sex with your spouse happens when you discover how to maximize each other's sexual pleasure.

Other Books By Dr. Jane Smart

The Simple Pregnancy Guide

Strong Woman: What It Means To Be A Woman Of Substance

Bonus Offer

The kindle edition will be available to you for FREE when you purchase the paperback version from Amazon.com (The US Store)

Have Fun Together

"Humor is the great thing, the saving thing. The minute it crops up, all our irritations and resentments slip away; a sunny spirit takes their place." – **Mark Twain**

Life can be so tough and demanding, and we all have such busy lives. While you and your spouse are busy rushing through life as you handle work, home, and children, remember to have fun with your spouse and create that time to be intimate and laugh with each other.

You can turn a boring and monotonous marriage into an interesting and lively relationship. Fulfilling each other's need for fun and excitement can rekindle the love in your marriage and bring back happiness and joy.

Think of the activities that excite you or your partner and do those things together. Successful marriages are not monotonous or boring.

Prioritize having fun and adventure with your spouse if you want to rekindle the love in your marriage. If you cannot find the time, look at how you spend time now. How many of those activities are more important than fun time with your spouse? How many of them are higher priorities for you than a successful marriage?

Put fun couple time ahead of other activities. Have frequent date nights, as mentioned previously. Go on an excursion. Resurrect the love and fun you had when you first got married.

Exercising together can increase the physical attraction between you and your spouse. It also creates an emotional bond, improves relationship satisfaction, and increases the love in your marriage. Register together at a gym or take a dance class with your spouse.

Laugh together. Have fun together. It is healthy to show those white teeth of yours. Being too serious is boring. Go on a journey together, just the two of you. Go on a date to your favorite restaurant. Take a cooking or language class together and learn something new.

Take a Vacation

"Sometimes I wonder if men and women really suit each other. Perhaps they should live next door and just visit now and then." – **Katharine Hepburn**

If work, kids, and other responsibilities have forced you and your spouse to put your love life aside, create some time off from all those responsibilities. Taking a vacation together can help you focus on each other and avoid the distractions of life's responsibilities.

If you have minor children, can they go to Grandma's so you and your mate can have a weekend or a vacation for just the two of you? Whether you go out of town or snuggle up in a staycation, time alone together in which you focus on each other without distractions can revitalize your marriage.

Before embarking on this vacation, you and your spouse should have an honest conversation about your expectations. Discuss what both of you aim to achieve with your vacation.

This important conversation should include how much time you and your spouse want to spend together, whether you plan to have more sex than usual, and what you and your spouse hope to achieve in terms of your relationship goals.

It may not seem romantic to lay out your entire plan ahead of time, but this will reduce the chance of you and your spouse feeling disappointed because you had different goals in mind for the vacation.

Spending quality time alone with your spouse without the kids and other responsibilities can help you remember the life you had when you were dating. Did you take trips together when you were dating? Did you spend entire weekends together? Do all the things that will make your spouse feel special and wanted and watch your relationship improve.

Practice Emotional Intimacy

"Love doesn't just sit there like stone; it has to be made, like bread, remade all the time, made new." –
Ursula K. Le Guin

A cute little phrase to help you remember the true meaning of intimacy is 'in-to-me, see.' This means seeing who your spouse really is underneath any façades or defenses presented to the world, and for your spouse to see you in the same way.

Dictionary.com defines intimacy as "showing a close union or combination of particles or elements: an intimate mixture." Being intimate involves mixing your life with the life of your spouse, a blending of souls and a sharing of hearts.

Human beings long for intimacy, for that connection to other people. We want someone to accept us after seeing us as we really are, without the need to pretend we are perfect. The relationship that most relies on intimacy is the one we have with our spouse.

Achieving real intimacy makes your spouse feel alive as if you had discovered him, as if you took the time to peer into the depths of his heart and soul. A lack of emotional intimacy in your marriage will make your spouse feel passed over and ignored.

If you decide in advance what you will see when you examine the life, soul, heart, and personality of your spouse, you may deny yourself that level of emotional intimacy that makes couples feel known to each other.

See your partner as she is, not as you expect or want her to be. Projecting your own needs and your own template for what a spouse should be, for what a man or woman should be, can blind you to your partner's best qualities and cause you to miss out on those individual nuances of heart, soul, and love that make your partner unique.

To build an intimate relationship with your spouse, you need to accept your spouse just as he is. Real intimacy can begin only when your spouse knows you and you know your spouse. Since intimacy means 'in-to-me, see,' your spouse needs to see in to you to discover who you are and to see your hopes, desires, fears, and dreams.

One important key that will make physical intimacy achievable is acceptance. Your spouse won't allow you to see into her heart and soul if you are judgmental, abusive, selfish, and unforgiving.

If you want your spouse to open his heart to you, you must give him a safe place to do so.

Another key factor of emotional intimacy is trust. Your partner must trust you to open up to you. Real emotional intimacy is impossible without this trust, and emotional intimacy is what keeps marriages thriving. You express emotional intimacy in a variety of ways.

Share and Reinforce Memories

"Spread love everywhere you go: first of all in your own house...let no one ever come to you without leaving better and happier. Be the living expression of God's kindness; kindness in your face, kindness in your eyes, kindness in your warm greeting." –

Mother Teresa

Resurrect the pet name you called your spouse when you were dating and newly married. Use endearments that you may not have uttered in years.

Spend a few moments writing down your memories of lovely times from your years together and from your wedding day. Include details about the tune that was 'your song' when you were dating, the one you heard countless times.

Surprise your spouse with the list. Your thoughtful gesture will endear you to her, and the list will help both of you remember why you married in the first place.

Spy on your spouse. Spend a few minutes observing your mate when he or she is unaware that you are watching, and use that observation as a prompt to write down ten things you love about your partner.

Maybe you love the sweet way he talks to you, the delicate way she eats, his great sense of humor, her lovely singing voice, the passion with which he shares the game he loves. Be reminded of all the things that you fell in love with and why you agreed to marry to marry in the first place.

Looking through old pictures depicting your history as a couple can remind you of why you fell in love. You can take it a step further by going through these relationship archives with your spouse and discussing the small and large moments that make up your life together.

Practice Acceptance and Tolerance

*"Happy marriages begin when we marry the ones we love, and they blossom when we love the ones we marry." – **Tom Mullen***

Maybe your spouse is not as articulate and open in expressing love as your best friend's spouse. Maybe your mate does not buy you flowers as regularly as your best friend's spouse. Perhaps your spouse has never written a love letter or love poem for you.

However, your spouse probably has a bazillion other ways to express how much he or she loves you. Think about how your spouse cares for you after a long day has beaten you down. Recall your mate's unique way of preparing your birthday breakfast. Look at how your partner treats the children you share. Think about the ways your spouse eases your burdens and shows tenderness and thoughtfulness.

When you find yourself brooding about the things your spouse does not do, always remember what he does do.

Do not try to read your spouse's mind. Often the biggest problem in a marriage comes from deciding what a spouse is thinking and doing without any evidence to back up the assumption. Unfounded jealousy is only one example of this.

Instead of getting angry because you assume that your partner does not want to go out with you or does not appreciate your efforts, ask what is actually going on in his or her head.

An easy way to rekindle love in your marriage is to stop assuming the worst. Talk it out. Humans are bound to commit errors, so expect less from your spouse. He or she cannot be perfect.

Compliment Your Spouse

"Water what you want to grow; don't water the weeds." – **A garden analogy**

After you have been married a long time, it is easy to see your spouse's negative traits. However, if you focus on those faults, the result will be hurt feelings and dissatisfaction between you and your spouse.

To rekindle the love in your marriage, avoid focusing on negative behavior and pay attention to the positive behavior of your spouse. Show appreciation for her actions that helped you rather than pointing out what she failed to do. Tell your spouse the things you love about him.

Whether the traits are intellectual, physical, or emotional, noticing them can help you see your spouse in a more positive way. To rekindle the love in your marriage, share more compliments while being more tolerant and accepting of traits you do not like.

When you give your spouse a flower, it is not the flower that makes her happy, but the intention behind the gift. By giving your spouse a flower, you announce to her and the world that you care about her.

Most people want attention from their spouses. Giving your partner a special gift tells him that you love him and consider him important.

Make it a priority to compliment your spouse regularly. Tell him that his clothes looks great on him. Acknowledge preparation of a good meal. Tell your spouse how much you love him often. Tell her how gorgeous she is. Provide some pampering; we all love that. Appreciation is an ego boost. Tell your spouse how proud you are to have him or her in your life.

Gratitude is an effective fuel to rekindle the love in your marriage. Tuck a note where your spouse will find it, letting her know how much you appreciate her. Touch your spouse on the arm and thank him for always being there for you.

Keep a gratitude journal, taking note every day of three attributes or actions of your spouse and marriage for which you are thankful.

Keep Communication Channels Open

"In every union there is a mystery." – **Henri F. Amiel**

Couples need to keep discussing things with each other, but too many couples stop communicating because they get so busy with their daily lives.

Do you and your spouse seem to be living like strangers under the same roof? Have you lost the connection you once had? Are you and your spouse so busy and involved with work and other responsibilities that you forget to talk intimately?

You need to reopen channels of communication to connect once again with each other. Try talking as you and your partner do housework or garden chores. Assisting your spouse with anything will create a channel of communication between the two of you.

Be willing to tell your partner what does and does not work for you romantically. Expressing how you feel and what you like saves your partner from guessing, and that increases intimacy.

Pouring love and attention into a project that you both have passion for can boost the love in your marriage. Creating something together—a charity organization or event, a business, or a garden—tends to increase the communication in your marriage.

Look for something that interests both of you. Spending time working on a project you both care about lets you see your spouse in a different light. It can help you remember what you love about her.

Take time to check in with your spouse several times per day and discuss personal matters more than family logistics. Communicating with your spouse will remind you both that you are lovers and not just co-parents or housemates.

Try this: Set an alarm to go off at a chosen time of day. When the alarm sounds, stop whatever you are doing and contact your spouse. Proper communication can solve many issues.

If your spouse did something that hurt you, whether it was a conscious or unconscious wounding, talk to your spouse about it instead of sulking. Always remember that your spouse cannot read your mind. If something bothers you, tell your spouse as quickly as possible. Use factual 'I statements' rather than blame—"I felt disregarded when you didn't call to say you would be late."

You also can express yourself in writing, especially if you do not feel articulate in expressing your thoughts and emotions verbally. Writing is a powerful way to communicate with your spouse. Thoughtful writing can help you avoid the regret of "That didn't come out the way I meant it" while also giving you a chance to say everything in your heart without being interrupted.

Putting your feelings on paper or a digital device can help you process them. Writing is a simple way to talk to yourself in silence.

Other Books By Dr. Jane Smart

<u>The Simple Pregnancy Guide</u>

<u>Strong Woman: What It Means To Be A Woman Of Substance</u>

Bonus Offer

The kindle edition will be available to you for FREE when you purchase the paperback version from Amazon.com (The US Store)

Break the Rules

"When you love, you wish to do things for. You wish to sacrifice for. You wish to serve." – **Ernest Hemingway**

Avoid being in a monotonous and boring relationship. This is very bad for a marriage. Monotony can lead to dissatisfaction and eventually serve as a reason for a divorce. Do something extraordinary and surprising every now and then. Stop leading a boring life or doing predictable things.

To rekindle the love in your marriage, try surprising your partner by acting differently. Plan an unexpected and unpredictable date with your spouse or buy a special gift for your mate that will add spontaneity, surprise, and fun to life. New experiences counter boredom.

Anything, anyhow, and anywhere works as long as it rekindles the love in your marriage.

Incorporating surprise into a marriage can rekindle love for relationships that have gone flat. Study your spouse and find ways to recapture the feeling of falling in love. Discover what triggers the rush of feel-good hormones (oxytocin and dopamine) for your spouse. Introduce surprise and novelty into your marriage.

You and your spouse can take turns on different weekends to plan a secret activity or visit different destinations for a special date. Use themes so that you avoid getting into a rut with date night. Themes could include a date with friends, a date at the beach, a date doing something neither of you has done before.

Honor Your Spouse's Preferences

"I love you not only for what you are, but for what I am when I am with you." – **Elizabeth Barrett**

You can make choices that you know your spouse prefers while still being true to yourself. Rekindle love by honoring your spouse's preferences whenever possible: Wear the haircut or hairstyle that your spouse loves. Dab on the perfume or cologne that pleases your mate. Dress for a date in the style that your spouse thinks looks best on you.

Whenever making a choice to please your partner will not violate the core of who you are as a person or add unreasonable stress to your day, choose to honor those preferences. You are not your hair, your nails, your beard, or your shirt.

If your partner says that you are brave, funny, or resourceful, you may find yourself becoming braver, funnier, or more resourceful. In a loving marriage, a mate can bring out our best characteristics.

Marriage gives us an opportunity to get to know each other so well that we understand what the other loves, looks for in other people, and regards as positive qualities.

Before we ever meet the person we marry, we have preferences about an ideal mate. Navigate your way into the mind of your partner to know his fantasies about a mate. Are there ways you can come closer to that ideal?

Doing what your spouse loves might require you to start practicing unusual things, but if doing so will bring joy and happiness into your marriage, why not?

Honoring your spouse's preferences whenever possible will reignite the fires of love and passion in your marriage.

Make Your Spouse Happy

"Always strive to give your spouse the very best of yourself; not what's left over after you have given your best to everyone else." – **Dave Willis**

You can find countless ways to make your spouse happy and glad that he or she is married to you. Introduce new things that will amaze your spouse; make your relationship an interesting one.

The accumulation of small things can make marriage great or terrible. Take time for those small, meaningful gestures that directly touch the heart and soul of your spouse.

Tell your spouse in words and deeds that no matter what happens, you will always be there for her. Do your best to improve yourself as well as your relationship. You should give the best of yourself to your spouse and be the best that you can be.

Happiness in a marriage starts within you. If you find it difficult to be happy with yourself, it will be harder for you to share happiness with your spouse. Your happiness is the best gift you can give to your partner.

To strengthen your marriage, increase the level of happiness in yourself and your relationship. Respect the personal decisions of your partner. Maintain balance in your life by working together as a family. Be the shoulder others can lean on. Avoid destructive criticism and fighting. Show your spouse that you have faith in him or her and be proud of your spouse's accomplishments.

Exhibit happiness when you are around your spouse. If you have a bright smile on your face, it will improve the mood for both of you. Being happy is a choice, so why choose to be sad? Make the world a brighter place by sharing your bright smile. Laugh aloud and joke around with your spouse. Watch funny movies together; share humorous content that you see online. Fill your married life with joy and happiness to maintain and sustain the love in your marriage.

Don't Argue in Anger

"If you will invest time listening, you will save that time in arguments." – **Joyce Meyer**

This next way to rekindle love probably will be the most difficult advice to adopt, but it will be the most effective when you do apply it: When you are angry with your partner, and you want to shout and scream and do something that is hurtful, just remain silent instead.

Have a rule with yourself that when your anger is in danger of becoming out of your control, you will always walk away from your spouse until the fury has cooled.

Words spoken in anger or actions taken in anger may poison your marriage. The actions or words might make you feel good in the moment, but they may cause irreparable harm to your marriage.

If you notice that a disagreement is escalating into a full-scale fight, excuse yourself from your spouse and finish the conversation when you have a cooler head.

If you want to get your angry feelings out without hurting your spouse, write down all the reasons you are angry and then tear up the list. Go for a run or a long walk and use that time to work through your feelings. Step aside from angry interactions to show that your relationship has a priority over your ego.

Disagreements can be healthy in a marriage, but they should not happen on a frequent basis. Never give disagreement a chance to eat away at your relationship. Always remember that no one ever wins in a marital fight; both parties lose. Argument can destroy a marriage.

When emotions are intense, you may say words that will be harmful to your spouse, even though you never meant to say them and may not believe them.

Always remember that you will not be able to take back hurtful words spoken in anger.

As much as possible, avoid intense arguments with your spouse. A fight easily can damage the love in your marriage. A disagreement might emanate from an unimportant matter, but before you both know it, it can escalate into a full-blown fight.

A key piece of advice is to avoid making an important decision when you are angry. You will likely regret decisions made in anger because anger makes it hard to think objectively.

Controlling your temper is very important in your marriage. (Of course, that is especially important if you ever resort to violence when you are angry; you may need professional help in that case.) When you are angry with your spouse, give yourself some time to cool down before acting. By avoiding acting immediately, you can prevent many hurtful arguments.

Limit Technology

"Turn off your email; turn off your phone; disconnect from the Internet; figure out a way to set limits so you can concentrate when you need to, and disengage when you need to. Technology is a good servant but a bad master." – **Gretchen Rubin**

We presently live in a world driven by technology. Many electronic gadgets have become part of our everyday lives. In the past decade, the technological advances available to humans have risen so fast that many marriages have crashed due to the negative effect of technology.

Many of these new technologies make communication easier. Electronic tools such as Gmail and Yahoo! Mail, WhatsApp, text messaging, and cell phones can make it easier to keep in touch with our mate even when we are apart.

However, the truth is that advances in technology seem to be causing problems for many couples.

Instead of helping communication, these electronic gadgets seem to pose a barrier to effective communication—and a sometimes-literal barrier between couples.

Instead of allowing for more time together, they seem to be taking away from quality time for many couples. Instead of making work easier and faster, technology seems to encourage many couples to take their work home with them, which further reduces communication with their spouse.

Technology is not inherently good or bad; how we use it makes it good, bad, or a mixture of both. Having access to the latest technology can help us live more easily and efficiently in the modern world, and technology does not have to be bad for your marriage.

However, the important step to avoid the negative effect of technology on your marriage is to set limits to technology use when you are with your spouse, to be the master of technology rather than its slave. Making a strong decision to address your usage of technology gadgets can enhance to your relationship.

If your spouse tries to communicate with you while you are watching your favorite program on TV, pause the program or stream it later so that you can listen to your spouse. Avoid sending text messages and checking social media while you are with your spouse, especially during dinner or while you are on a date together.

To rekindle the love in your marriage, you need to set aside technology to create adequate time for your spouse. When you are spending time with your spouse (as opposed to merely being in the same space), give him or her your full attention instead of multitasking with your gadgets.

You and your spouse should decide together how much time is reasonable to spend on electronics daily. For example, two hours of TV time may be a good limit for one couple, but you and your spouse may decide one hour a day is enough given your priorities and commitments.

Set your technology limits depending on your schedules and responsibilities; a retired couple will not need the same limits as a couple juggling work, education, and childcare.

Before you make any changes, spend a week making daily notes about how much time you spend calling, texting, streaming entertainment, playing video games, watching TV, being on social media, and surfing the internet.

This week of data is a revelation for many couples. Many of us underestimate how much time we spend using our electronic devices each day; you may be surprised to discover how many hours you actually spend in the virtual world.

Once you know how much time you and your spouse actually spend using technology, develop a plan with your mate to decrease your usage if it is excessive. Spend the time gained in talking to your spouse or being active together.

When you are geographically apart, technology can help you stay connected to your spouse. For other times, instead of communicating with your spouse through WhatsApp, text messages, calls, or social media, spend more time together.

Let real face time with your spouse replace FaceTime. A date night can replace television time. Get outside with your spouse and spend time together in nature. Find something you can do together that will help you to build your marriage with love so that electronics become less important.

The two of you should leave your cell phones at home when you are together. If you think you cannot do this, just remember that until about two decades ago, people did not have mobile phones and survived just fine.

If you cannot leave your mobile phones for valid reasons, at least agree to mute them and avoid constantly checking to see if you missed anything. The point here is to give your spouse your undivided attention.

Have A Happy Married Life!

"Grow old along with me. The best is yet to be."

– Robert Browning

With knowledge about the twenty ways to rekindle your marriage gained from reading this book, you and your spouse can face challenges whatever they may be.

If love, joy, and happiness have disappeared from your marriage, are you ready to do something about it?

Always keep in mind that love is like fire: if you do not add fuel to the fire, it will go out. To keep the fire of love burning perpetually in your marriage, improve communications with your spouse and create an avenue to show your spouse how much you care.

Your marriage is the reason that you work hard for a living. It gave you a foundation for parenthood if you have children. You cannot neglect your marriage for work, kids, and other responsibilities. You need to balance your time to reflect that your marriage is a high priority for you.

Talk out the problems in your marriage and commit to change for the better. Stop complaining and focus instead on positive outcomes.

An easy way to rekindle the love in your marriage is to remember interesting things you and your spouse used to do when you first married and start doing those things again.

It is important to understand that the love that once flourished between you and your spouse is unlikely to have disappeared. Instead, the weight of displeasure, desertion, abandonment, resentment, and loneliness has submerged love and passion. You can easily rekindle the love in your marriage if you are ready to do the work.

If you value the love between you and your spouse and you do not want to lose it, you and your spouse need to take the initiative to overcome these challenges.

Give your spouse this book to read and discuss together how you can place your marriage as the number one priority in your life. Discuss with your spouse ways in which you can express your love by showing more respect and kindness and by having more fun together.

The End

Thank you very much for taking the time to read this book. If you found this book useful please let me know by leaving a review on Amazon! Reviews are the lifeblood of independent authors. Your support really does make a difference and I read all the reviews personally so I can get your feedback and make this book even better.

If you did not like this book, then please tell me! Email me at **DrJaneSmart@yahoo.com** and let me know what you didn't like. Perhaps I can change it. In today's world a book doesn't have to be stagnant, it can improve with time and feedback from readers like you.

You can impact this book, and I welcome your feedback. Help make this book better for everyone!

Thanks again for your support!

Other Books By Dr. Jane Smart

The Simple Pregnancy Guide

Strong Woman: What It Means To Be A Woman Of Substance

Bonus Offer

The kindle edition will be available to you for FREE when you purchase the paperback version from Amazon.com (The US Store)

www.ingramcontent.com/pod-product-compliance
Lightning Source LLC
Chambersburg PA
CBHW062109280426
43661CB00086B/397